Fun with Spot

Written by Cassandra Belton
Illustrated by Joseph Green

Phonics Skills

Short a			Short e	Short i		
can	fast	lap	pet	big	will	hill
had				dig	in	did
				sip	if	it
				sit		

Short o			Short u		
Spot	not	lot	pup	run	fun
hot	on	top	up	mud	tug
			hug	jump	

Spot is my pup.
Spot is not a big pet.

Spot can run fast.
Spot will run for fun.
Spot will run up the hill.

Spot can dig.
Spot will dig in the mud.
Spot will dig up a lot of mud.

Spot can tug.
I will tug with Spot.
What did Spot tug?

Spot can sip.
If it is hot,
Spot will sip a lot.

Spot can sit.
Spot will sit on my lap
on top of the hill.

I will hug Spot.
Spot had fun.
We will jump up.